A World of Homes

by Amy Baker

Designer: Meredith Smith

Credits: cover ©Nancy Brown/Photographer's Choice/Getty; **1** (bg) ©iStockphoto.com/edge69; **2** ©Jupiterimages/Brand X Pictures/Thinkstock; **3** (c) ©Alamy, (tr) ©Tranz/Corbis; **4-5** (c) ©Inside-photo/Erick Saillet/Getty, (tr) ©Inside-photo/Erick Saillet/Getty; **6** ©Tranz/Corbis; **7** ©Alamy; **8** ©Alamy; **9** ©Alamy; **10-11** (c) ©iStockphoto.com/molloykeith, (tr) ©Alamy; **12** ©Geoff Dann/Dorling Kindersley/Getty; **13** ©iStockphoto.com/TimothyBall; **14-15** (c) ©Alamy, (tr) ©Alamy; **16** ©Shutterstock/Stephen Coburn.

ISBN-13: 978-0-545-28901-6
ISBN-10: 0-545-28901-7

SCHOLASTIC INC.

New York   Toronto   London   Auckland   Sydney   New Delhi   Hong Kong

A home is where you
live with your family.

Do you like high places?
You could live in a tall building
made of bricks.

Do you like to look outside?
You could live in a home
made of glass.
You can see all around in a glass house.

Do you like to keep cool
when it's hot?
You could live in a home
made of mud.
Mud houses are cool
on hot days.

Do you like to be in the woods?
You could live in a tree house.
You could live in a home
made of logs and leaves.

Do you like to move
from place to place?
You could live in a yurt.
You could take your home with you.

Yurts are made of felt and wood.
They can be put up
in one day.
And they can be taken down
and moved to a new place.

Do you like old places?
You could live in a home
made long ago.
You could live in a castle
made of stone.

Do you like the water?
You could live in a home
on the water.
You could live in a houseboat.

A home is where you live
with your family.
What kind of home do you like?